Snow Leopards

by Erika L. Shores

Consulting Editor: Gail Saunders-Smith, PhD

Consultant: Robin Keith
Senior Research Coordinator
San Diego Zoo's Institute for Conservation Research

CAPSTONE PRESS
a capstone imprint

Pebble Plus is published by Capstone Press,
151 Good Counsel Drive, P.O. Box 669, Mankato, Minnesota 56002.
www.capstonepub.com

Books published by Capstone Press are manufactured with paper
containing at least 10 percent post-consumer waste.

Library of Congress Cataloging-in-Publication Data
Shores, Erika L., 1976–
  Snow leopards / by Erika L. Shores.
  p. cm.—(Pebble plus. Wildcats)
  Includes bibliographical references and index.
  Summary: "Simple text and full-color photos explain the habitat, life cycle, range, and behavior of snow
leopards"—Provided by publisher.
  ISBN 978-1-4296-4483-9 (library binding)
  1. Snow leopard—Juvenile literature. I. Title. II. Series.
QL737.C23S5458 2011
599.75'55—dc22   2010002800

Editorial Credits
Katy Kudela, editor; Bobbie Nuytten, designer; Svetlana Zhurkin, media researcher; Eric Manske, production specialist

Photo Credits
Alamy/Purple Pilchards, 16–17
Creatas, back cover, 7, 12–13, 21
Dreamstime/Pawel Kotarba, 1
Peter Arnold/Biosphoto/J.-L. Klein & M.-L. Hubert, 5, 9; Biosphoto/Pierre Vernay, 15; H. Reinhard, 19; Wildlife, 11
Photo Researchers/Tom & Pat Leeson, cover
Shutterstock/Fenton (paw prints), cover and throughout

The author dedicates this book to her daughter, Erin Marie Shores.

Note to Parents and Teachers

The Wildcats series supports national science standards related to life science. This book
describes and illustrates snow leopards. The images support early readers in understanding
the text. The repetition of words and phrases helps early readers learn new words. This book
also introduces early readers to subject-specific vocabulary words, which are defined in the
Glossary section. Early readers may need assistance to read some words and to use the Table of
Contents, Glossary, Read More, Internet Sites, and Index sections of the book.

Printed in the United States of America in North Mankato, Minnesota.
012011   006047R

Table of Contents

Spotted in the Snow

A snow leopard creeps

across the snowy mountains.

This wildcat is hard to see.

It blends in with the

snow and rocks.

Snow leopards live

in central Asia.

They make their homes

on rocky mountain cliffs.

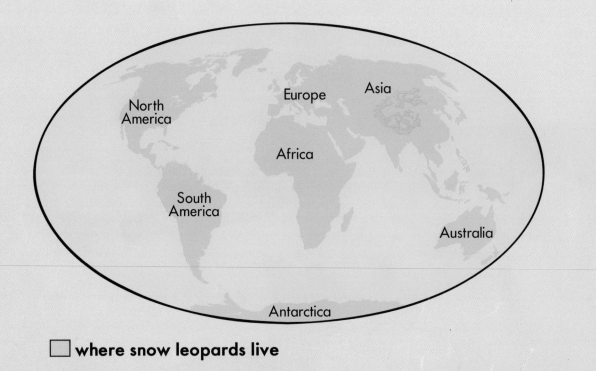

where snow leopards live

Snow Leopard Bodies

Snow leopards have

stocky bodies.

They weigh up to

121 pounds (55 kilograms).

house cat

snow leopard

Thick fur keeps
snow leopards warm.
Snow leopards use
their long, fluffy tails
like a scarf.

Good Hunters

Snow leopards are quick hunters.

Their strong back legs

help them leap from cliffs.

Their wide paws keep them

on top of snow as they run.

In the Himalaya mountains,

snow leopards stalk wild sheep.

In other parts of Asia,

they hunt goats,

marmots, and pikas.

Snow Leopard Life Cycle

In the spring, females
give birth to litters
of two or three cubs.
By three months, cubs are
ready to learn how to hunt.

At around 20 months, young
leopards leave their mothers.
Adult cats live alone.
They use claw marks and
smells to mark their ranges.

Snow leopards are endangered.
Government laws try to keep
them safe from hunters.
If left alone, snow leopards can
live up to 18 years in the wild.

Glossary

cliff—a high, steep rock face

endangered—in danger of dying out; today there are fewer than 7,000 snow leopards living in Asia

litter—a group of animals born at the same time to one mother

marmot—a rodent with a stocky body, short legs, stiff fur, and bushy tail; a marmot looks like a woodchuck

pika—a small, short-eared mammal that looks like a small guinea pig

range—an area where an animal naturally lives

stalk—to hunt an animal in a quiet, secret way

stocky—a short, heavy build

Read More

Hatkoff, Craig. *Leo, the Snow Leopard.* New York: Scholastic Press, 2010.

Pitts, Zachary. *The Pebble First Guide to Wildcats.* Pebble First Guides. Mankato, Minn.: Capstone Press, 2009.

Internet Sites

FactHound offers a safe, fun way to find Internet sites related to this book. All of the sites on FactHound have been researched by our staff.

Here's all you do:

Visit *www.facthound.com*

FactHound will fetch the best sites for you!

Index

Word Count: 185

Grade: 1

Early-Intervention Level: 17